MW00893385

This book belongs to:

Made in the USA
Las Vegas, NV
09 December 2022

61547226R00070